The Easy Tin Whistle Praise-and-Worship Book

30 Timeless Hymns by Women Composers of Old-Time American Christian Music with Tabs and Chords in the Bluegrass Keys of D and G

Online MP3

Arranged by

Peter Upclaire

Peter Upclaire

The Easy Tin Whistle Praise-and-Worship Book

30 Timeless Hymns by Women Composers of
Old-Time American Christian Music
with Tabs and Chords
in the Bluegrass Keys of D and G

- Lovely melodies from the past -

First edition: May, 2023

Available from Amazon.com and other book stores.

Copyright © 2023 Peter Upclaire

More information about other books can be found at
www.lovelymelodies.com.

Online MP3

Contents

Introduction

Christian hymnody has a rich and diverse history in the United States. While many hymns are well-known, the contributions of female composers have often been overlooked. This book will show the remarkable and inspiring work of female composers of old-time American Christian hymns from the 19th and early 20th centuries. Despite their time's social and cultural challenges, these women crafted beautiful hymns that have stood the test of time and continue to be cherished by believers today.

Through this collection of 30 hymns, arranged for instruments such as guitar, mandolin, ukulele, and others, we aim to shine a light on the rich musical legacy of these female composers. Each hymn is presented with tabs and chords, making it accessible for musicians of all skill levels to play and enjoy. Whether you are a worship leader, a musician, or simply a hymn enthusiast, this book provides a unique opportunity to explore the works of these talented women and experience their music in a new way.

The hymns in this book reflect a wide range of themes, including faith, salvation, grace, hope, and more. They offer profound expressions of devotion, praise, and worship. They are a testament to the enduring power of music in conveying deep spiritual truths. From the timeless classics of Fanny Crosby to the lesser-known gems of Charlotte Alington and Sarah Geraldina Stock, each hymn in this collection showcases these female composers' unique voices and perspectives.

Beyond their musical contributions, these women's lives are also inspiring testimonies of faith, resilience, and creativity. They broke societal barriers and pushed against the limitations placed on them as women in their time, using their gifts to express their faith and impact the world through their music. Their stories are a testament to the power of music to transcend social boundaries and bring people together in worship.

As you journey through the pages of this book, may you be inspired by the music and stories of these remarkable women. And may their hymns continue to inspire and uplift the hearts of believers for generations to come.

The era between 1850 and 1900

The era between 1850 and 1900 in the United States was a transformative period marked by significant social, political, economic, and technological changes. It was a time of rapid industrialization, westward expansion, and societal shifts that shaped the nation's history.

During this era, the United States experienced a surge in industrialization, with the growth of railroads, factories, and urban centers. This led to the rise of big business and the consolidation of wealth, as well as significant changes in the economy and labor force. Industrialization brought about advancements in transportation, communication, and manufacturing, leading to increased production and urbanization.

The country also witnessed major social changes during this time. The issue of slavery came to a head, leading to the American Civil War, a bloody conflict that resulted in the abolition of slavery with the passage of the 13th Amendment to the Constitution. The Reconstruction Era followed, marked by efforts to rebuild and reunify the nation, but also fraught with challenges and social tensions.

The era was also marked by westward expansion, with the completion of the Transcontinental Railroad in 1869, opening up new opportunities for settlement and economic growth in the western frontier. This era witnessed the rapid development of cities and the growth of urban populations, as people migrated from rural areas to seek employment in factories and industries.

Culturally, the era saw the emergence of new artistic and literary movements, such as the Romanticism and Realism literary movements, and the rise of American authors such as Mark Twain, Emily Dickinson, and Walt Whitman. Music, theater, and visual arts also flourished during this time, reflecting the changing times and societal shifts. But it was also the time of the rise of Christian values.

Christian hymns

Christian hymns played a significant role in the religious and cultural landscape of the United States during the 19th century. These hymns, often sung in churches and religious gatherings, reflected the time's spiritual beliefs, social values, and musical traditions.

One of the prominent characteristics of Christian hymns in the 19th century was their emphasis on traditional Christian doctrines and teachings. Many of these hymns focused on themes such as salvation, grace, redemption, and the love of God, reflecting the strong influence of evangelical Christianity that prevailed during this era.

The hymns of this period were typically characterized by simple melodies and lyrics that were easy to sing and memorize. They often featured four-part harmonies, with a melody line and three supporting harmonies. They were accompanied by piano, organ, or other musical instruments.

Many Christian hymns composed during this era were written by notable hymn writers, such as Fanny Crosby, Philip Bliss, and Isaac Watts. These hymn writers often drew from their own personal experiences and struggles, as well as from Scripture, to craft meaningful and powerful hymns that resonated with the religious sentiments of the time.

Christian hymns in the 19th century also served as social and cultural expression. They were sung in churches, camp meetings, revivals, and other gatherings, fostering community and shared faith among believers. Hymns were also used in the abolitionist and temperance movements and in the fight for women's suffrage, providing a spiritual and moral foundation for social reform efforts of the time.

Overall, Christian hymns in the 19th century in the United States were an integral part of the religious and cultural fabric of the era, as they played a significant role in social and cultural movements of the time.

Women in hymn writing and hymn composition

The role and position of women in hymn writing and composition during the 19th century in the United States were complex and multifaceted. While women made significant contributions to Christian hymnody during this time, they faced various challenges and limitations due to their gender.

One notable aspect of the role of women in hymn writing during the 19th century was their active participation in hymn composition. Women like Fanny Crosby, Sarah Flower Adams, and Julia Ward Howe, among others, wrote hymns that became widely popular and are still sung today. These women often drew from their personal experiences, faith, and theological convictions.

Moreover, women's involvement in hymn writing was often tied to their roles as wives, mothers, and homemakers. The prevailing societal norms and cultural expectations of the time often relegated women to domestic roles and limited their opportunities for public engagement. Women were not allowed to preach, and their contributions to hymnody were often overlooked or attributed to male collaborators.

Despite these challenges, women's hymn writing in the 19th century significantly impacted the religious and cultural landscape of the United States. Their hymns provided a unique perspective on faith, spirituality, and social issues. They often addressed suffering, redemption, and social justice themes. Women's hymns also played a significant role in the burgeoning women's suffrage movement, providing a platform for women's voices and advocating for gender equality.

In conclusion, the role and position of women in hymn writing and composition during the 19th century in the United States were marked by both contributions and limitations. Women contributed significantly to Christian hymnody but faced societal constraints and gender biases. However, their hymns continue to be cherished and sung today, reflecting the enduring impact of their work on the Christian worship tradition.

Beyond the music, the stories of these female composers are also a testament to their faith, resilience, and creativity in the face of societal barriers. And now, it is time to capture a glimpse into their lives and musical contributions, showcasing their enduring impact on Christian hymnody in America.

Women Composers of Old-Time American Christian Music

Clara H. Scott

Clara H. Scott (1841 - 1897) was a renowned American composer of Christian hymns in the 19th century. Her hymns are characterized by her deep relationship with God and dedication to the Christian faith. Her lyrics and music are recognized for their poetic and musical quality and their ability to continue inspiring believers on their spiritual journey.

In addition to composing, Clara H. Scott was known as a music educator and arranger of other compositions. Her arrangements were often used in music lessons due to her ability to make complex musical concepts accessible to students. She was highly esteemed for her music theory expertise and contributions to music education in the United States.

The hymns of Clara H. Scott have had a lasting impact on Christian worship, as her compositions are still appreciated worldwide. One of Clara H. Scott's significant achievements is her composition "Open My Eyes, That I May See." With its heartfelt lyrics and soul-stirring melody, this hymn is still included in numerous hymnals and sung in churches.

Eliza Edmunds Hewitt

Eliza Edmunds Hewitt (1851 - 1920) was a prolific American composer of Christian hymns in the late 19th and early 20th centuries. Her hymns, known for their heartfelt and inspiring lyrics, accompanied by memorable and melodic tunes, are still highly regarded today.

Hewitt began her career as a teacher and educator but turned to hymn writing after being bedridden for an extended period due to a serious illness. Her hymns expressed her deep faith and trust in God. Due to the versatility of her hymns, they were sung in various Christian denominations, and her compositions were included in hymnals used in different Christian schools, where both children and adults would sing them.

Fanny Crosby

Fanny Crosby (1820 - 1915), born Frances Jane van Alstyne, is one of the most renowned American hymnists and composers of Christian songs. Despite being blind from childhood due to a childhood illness and losing her father in her youth, Crosby's talent for writing hymns emerged early in her life.

Crosby wrote over 8,000 hymns in her long career, making her one of history's most prolific hymn writers. Her hymns are known for their rich theology, poetic language, and deep emotions.

In addition to hymn writing, Crosby advocated for blind people and tirelessly worked to improve their well-being. She was a prominent public figure, poet, and writer and met with Presidents Grover Cleveland and Benjamin Harrison. She knew and collaborated with esteemed musicians of her time, such as William Bradbury and Ira Sankey.

Her most famous composition, "Blessed Assurance," has become a beloved classic in Christian worship, and millions worldwide still sing it today.

Lucy Rider Meyer

Lucy Rider Meyer (1849–1922) was a prolific composer of Christian hymns. She was known for hymns that expressed deep spiritual truths and conveyed messages of faith and hope. Her hymns are characterized by lyrical depth and poetic imagery, often reflecting her experiences and struggles.

Meyer was also known for her passionate preaching, writing, and teaching on holiness, social justice, and women's rights.

Meyer's hymns were published in various hymnals during her lifetime, and Christians worldwide still sing them today. Her hymns are recognizable for their musical beauty and messages of faith and social justice.

Margaret J. Harris

Despite her relatively short life, Margaret J. Harris (1865 - 1919) is known for her contributions to Christian hymnody. Her lyrics are filled with emotional depths and spiritual insights, while her melodies are known for their musical beauty. In short, her compositions, with her exceptional approach, often inspired and uplifted those who sang them during worship.

Her hymns were published in various hymnals and remained a cherished part of the Christian hymnody. They are known for their spiritual depth, musical beauty, and enduring messages of faith and devotion.

Mary Artemisia Lathbury

Mary Artemisia Lathbury (1841 - 1913) expressed her deep faith and love for God through her hymns. Her songs are filled with poetic language, and she drew messages from her personal experiences and deep understanding of the Holy Scriptures. Her lyrics often drew from natural imagery to convey spiritual truths and evoke a sense of wonder and awe for God's work.

Her hymns were frequently published in hymnals and sung in churches across the United States. Due to their rich imagery and sincere expressions of worship, her music continues to inspire and uplift the hearts of believers to this day.

Mary C. Seward

Mary C. Seward (1839 - 1919) was a renowned American hymnist and composer of Christian songs, particularly known for her hymn lyrics. Her lyrics often focus on praise, thanksgiving, and surrendering to God's will. In addition to hymn writing, Seward was a composer and actively involved in various Christian ministries and missionary work.

Her music was frequently published in hymnals and continues to be sung in churches throughout the United States.

Matilda T. Durham

Matilda T. Durham (1815 - 1901) is another notable American hymnist and composer of Christian songs in the 19th century. Although little is known about her life, her contributions to Christian music have left a lasting impact. Her hymns are characterized by sincere lyrics and melodic melodies. Her compositions were often featured in popular hymnals of her time and sung in churches throughout the United States.

While Durham's works may be relatively lesser known than some of her contemporaries, her hymns were highly esteemed for their poetic and musical excellence. Her compositions were known to inspire and uplift believers, and her music can still be encountered in various churches today.

Phoebe Knapp

Phoebe Knapp (1839 - 1908) was a renowned American hymnist and composer of Christian songs in the 19th century. Knapp's musical talent was evident from a young age, and she began composing hymns and playing the piano at an early stage. Her hymns were known for their melodic richness and ability to convey deep spiritual truths.

In addition to writing hymns, Knapp was a successful pianist and music teacher. She traveled extensively, giving concerts and teaching music. Her performances were highly regarded for her exceptional piano skills and ability to captivate audiences with her music.

One of the most significant events in Knapp's life was her collaboration with writer and composer Fanny Crosby. Their hymns were frequently published in hymnals and became popular in churches across the United States and beyond. Knapp's hymns continue to be sung in churches worldwide.

Hymns

All for Jesus

Mary D. James (1810 - 1883) Phoebe Palmer Knapp (1839 – 1908)

All for Jesus! All for Jesus!
All my being's ransomed pow'rs,
all my thoughts and words and doings,
all my days and all my hours.

Refrain 1:
All for Jesus! All for Jesus!
All my days and all my hours;
All for Jesus! All for Jesus!
All my days and all my hours.

Let my hands perform his bidding,
let my feet run in his ways;
let my eyes see Jesus only,
let my lips speak forth his praise.

Refrain 2:
All for Jesus! All for Jesus!
Let my lips speak forth His praise;
All for Jesus! All for Jesus!
Let my lips speak forth His praise.

Since my eyes were fixed on Jesus,
I've lost sight of all beside;
so enchained my spirit's vision,
looking at the Crucified.

Refrain 3:
All for Jesus! All for Jesus!
Looking at the Crucified;
All for Jesus! All for Jesus!
Looking at the Crucified.

O what wonder! How amazing!
Jesus, glorious King of kings,
deigns to call me his beloved,
lets me rest beneath his wings.

Refrain 4:
All for Jesus! All for Jesus!
Resting now beneath His wings;
All for Jesus! All for Jesus!
Resting now beneath His wings.

Behold Me Standing at the Door

Fanny Crosby (1820 – 1915)

Phoebe Palmer Knapp (1839 – 1908)

Behold me standing at the door,
And hear me pleading evermore
With gentle voice: O heart of sin,
May I come in? May I come in?

Refrain:
Behold me standing at the door,
And hear me pleading evermore:
Say, weary heart, oppressed with sin,
May I come in? May I come in?

I bore the cruel thorns for thee,
I waited long and patiently;
Say, weary heart, oppressed with sin,
May I come in? May I come in?

I would not plead with thee in vain;
Remember all my grief and pain;
I died to ransom thee from sin,
May I come in? May I come in?

I bring thee joy from Heaven above,
I bring thee pardon, peace and love;
Say, weary heart, oppressed with sin,
May I come in? May I come in?

Blessed Assurance

Frances Jane van Alstyne (1820 – 1915)

Phoebe Palmer Knapp (1839 – 1908)

16

Blessed assurance, Jesus is mine!
Oh, what a foretaste of glory divine!
Heir of salvation, purchase of God,
born of his Spirit, washed in his blood.

Refrain:
This is my story, this is my song,
praising my Savior all the day long.
This is my story, this is my song,
praising my Savior all the day long.

Perfect communion, perfect delight,
visions of rapture now burst on my sight.
Angels descending bring from above
echoes of mercy, whispers of love.

Perfect submission, all is at rest.
I in my Savior am happy and bless'd,
watching and waiting, looking above,
filled with his goodness, lost in his love.

The Cleansing Wave

Phoebe Palmer Knapp (1839 – 1908)

Oh, now I see the crimson wave!
The fountain deep and wide;
Jesus, my Lord, mighty to save,
Points to His wounded side.

Refrain:
The cleansing stream I see, I see!
I plunge, and, oh, it cleanseth me!
Oh, praise the Lord, it cleanseth me!
It cleanseth me, yes, cleanseth me.

I see the new creation rise,
I hear the speaking blood;
It speaks, polluted nature dies,
Sinks 'neath the cleansing flood.

I rise to walk in Heav'n's own light,
Above the world and sin,
With heart made pure and garments white,
And Christ enthroned within.

Amazing grace! 'tis Heav'n below
To feel the blood applied,
And Jesus, only Jesus know,
My Jesus crucified.

Come With Rejoicing, Come With Delight

Fanny Crosby (1820 - 1915)   Phoebe Palmer Knapp (1839 – 1908)

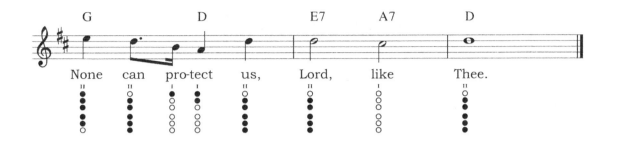

Come with rejoicing, come with delight,
Nature in waking, glad and bright;
Hearts overflowing gather today,
Fill us with rapture, Lord we pray.

Refrain:
Praise our Redeemer, tell of His love,
Praise our Redeemer, God above;
Tell of His mercy, boundless and free,
None can protect us, Lord, like Thee;
Tell of His mercy, boundless and free,
None can protect us, Lord, like Thee.

Guarded from danger, sheltered and blest,
Under His banner, calm, we rest,
Come we before Him, come with a song,
Tell how He leads us all day long.

Oh! what a Savior, gracious to all,
Oh! how His blessings round us fall,
Gently to comfort, kindly to cheer,
Sleeping or waking, God is near.

Still may His mercy tenderly flow,
Still may He guide us here below;
Then when our journey safely is past,
May we be gathered home at last.

Consecration

Mary D. James (1810-1883)

Pheobe Palmer Knapp (1839 – 1908)

♩ = 130

My bod - y, soul and spir - it, Je - sus, I give to thee, A

con - se - crat - ed of - fering, Thine ev - er - more to be. My

all is on the al - tar, I'm wait - for the fire;

Wait-ing, wait-ing, wait - ing, I'm wait - ing for the fire.

My body, soul and spirit,
Jesus, I give to thee,
A consecrated offering,
Thine evermore to be.

Refrain:
My all is on the altar,
I'm waiting for the fire;
Waiting, waiting, waiting,
I'm waiting for the fire.

O Jesus, mighty Saviour,
I trust in thy great name;
I look for thy salvation,
Thy promise now I claim.

O let the fire, descending
Just now upon my soul,
Consume my humble offering,
And cleanse and make me whole!

I'm thine, O blessèd Jesus,
Washed by thy precious blood;
Now seal me by thy Spirit
A sacrifice to God.

Enter In

Mary C. Seward (1839 – 1919)

Why shouldst thou longer knock
At the door of my soul?
Dear Saviour, enter in:
Thou alone canst make me whole.

Refrain:
Enter in, enter in
At the door of my soul;
Enter in, blessed Lord:
Thou alone canst make me whole.

I know thou art the life,
Flowing full, flowing free;
Come, Jesus, and abide;
All my hopes are fixed on thee.

Oh, hide my life in thine,
Let me seek but thy will,
All self to sacrifice,
And thy law of love fulfill.

God Is Love

Clara H. Scott (1841 - 1897)

God is Love; that Love surrounds me,
In that Love I safely dwell,
'Tis above, beneath, within me,
Love is mine, and all is well.
God is Love, pure Love,
God is Love, sweet Love,
That Love is mine—mine
And all is well.

God is Life; that Life surrounds me,
In that Life I safely dwell,
'Tis above, beneath, within me,
Life is mine, and all is well.
God is Life, pure Life,
God is Life, sweet Life,
That Life is mine—mine
And all is well.

God is Health; that Health surrounds me,
In that Health I safely dwell,
'Tis above, beneath, within me,
Health is mine, and all is well.
God is Health, pure Health,
God is Health, sweet Health,
That Health is mine—mine
And all is well.

God is Peace; that Peace surrounds me,
In that Peace I safely dwell,
'Tis above, beneath, within me,
Peace is mine, and all is well.
God is Peace, pure Peace,
God is Peace, sweet Peace,
That Peace is mine—mine
And all is well.

God is Strength; that Strength surrounds me,
In that Strength I safely dwell,
'Tis above, beneath, within me,
Strength is mine, and all is well.
God is Strength, pure Strength,
God is Strength, sweet Strength,
That Strength is mine—mine,
And all is well.

God is Joy; that Joy surrounds me,
In that Joy I safely dwell,
'Tis above, beneath, within me,
Joy is mine, and all is well.
God is Joy, pure Joy,
God is Joy, sweet Joy,
That Joy is mine—mine
And all is well.

God is Truth; that Truth surrounds me,
In that Truth I safely dwell,
'Tis above, beneath, within me,
Truth is mine, and all is well.
God is Truth, pure Truth,
God is Truth, sweet Truth,
That Truth is mine—mine
And all is well.

He Took My Sins Away

Margaret J. Harris (1865 - 1919)

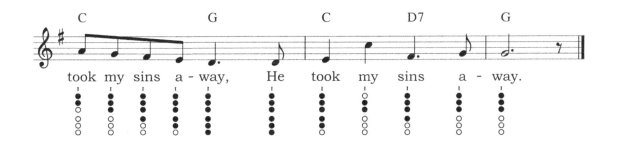

I came to Jesus, weary, worn, and sad,
He took my sins away, He took my sins away;
And now His love has made my heart so glad,
He took my sins away.

Refrain:
He took my sins away, He took my sins away,
And keeps me singing ev'ry day!
I'm so glad He took my sins away,
He took my sins away.

The load of sin was more than I could bear,
He took them all away, He took them all away;
And now on Him I roll my ev'ry care,
He took my sins away.

No condemnation have I in my heart,
He took my sins away, He took my sins away;
His perfect peace He did to me impart,
He took my sins away.

If you will come to Jesus Christ today,
He'll take your sins away, He'll take your sins away;
And keep you happy in His love each day,
He'll take your sins away.

He Was Not Willing

Lucy Rider Meyer (1849 - 1922)

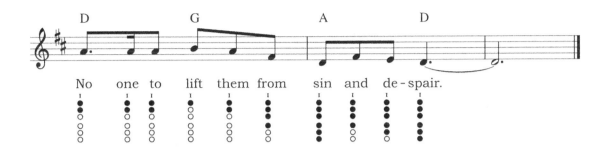

No one to lift them from sin and de-spair.

He was not willing that any should perish;
Jesus enthroned in the glory above,
Saw our poor fallen world, pitied our sorrows,
Poured out His life for us, wonderful love!
Perishing, perishing! Thronging our pathway,
Hearts break with burdens too heavy to bear:
Jesus would save, but there's no one to tell them,
No one to lift them from sin and despair.

He was not willing that any should perish;
Clothed in our flesh with its sorrow and pain,
Came He to seek the lost, comfort the mourner,
Heal the heart broken by sorrow and shame.
Perishing, perishing! Harvest is passing,
Reapers are few and the night draweth near:
Jesus is calling thee, haste to the reaping,
Thou shalt have souls, precious souls for thy hire.

Plenty for pleasure, but little for Jesus;
Time for the world with its troubles and toys,
No time for Jesus' work, feeding the hungry,
Lifting lost souls to eternity's joys.
Perishing, perishing! Hark, how they call us;
Bring us your Savior, oh, tell us of Him!
We are so weary, so heavily laden,
And with long weeping our eyes have grown dim.

He was not willing that any should perish;
Am I His follower, and can I live
Longer at ease with a soul going downward,
Lost for the lack of the help I might give!
Perishing, perishing! Thou wast not willing;
Master, forgive, and inspire us anew;
Banish our worldliness, help us to ever
Live with eternity's values in view.

I Am so Glad

Clara H. Scott (1841 - 1897)

I am so glad that Jesus taught How God loves me,
I am so glad that ne'er a frown On His face I'll see.

Refrain:
Sing hallelujah, hallelujah, glad, glad am I,
Sing hallelujah, hallelujah, glad, glad am I!

I am so glad that safely I May trust His care,
Finding in Him a perfect freedom From sin's false snare.

I am so glad that Jesus lived And proved the way,
Sweetest release from ev'ry sorrow To find alway.

I am so glad that Death has lost His vaunted pow'r;
Jesus has conquered, so may I In my passing hour.

In a Little While We're Going Home

Eliza Edmunds Hewitt (1851 – 1920)

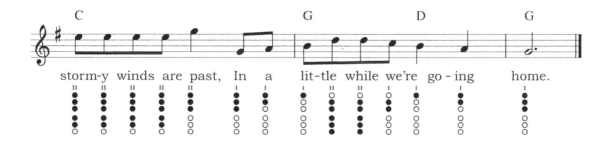

storm-y winds are past, In a lit-tle while we're go - ing home.

Let us sing a song that will cheer us by the way,
In a little while we're going home;
For the night will end in the everlasting day,
In a little while we're going home.

Refrain
In a little while, in a little while,
We shall cross the billow's foam;
We shall meet at last,
When the stormy winds are past,
In a little while we're going home.

We will do the work that our hands may find to do,
In a little while we're going home;
And the grace of God will our daily strength renew,
In a little while we're going home.

We will smooth the path for some weary, way-worn feet,
In a little while we're going home;
And may loving hearts spread around an influence sweet!
In a little while we're going home.

There's a rest beyond, there's relief from every care,
In a little while we're going home;
And no tears shall fall in that city bright and fair,
In a little while we're going home.

I Do Not Walk Alone

Mary O. Page

Clara H. Scott (1841 - 1897)

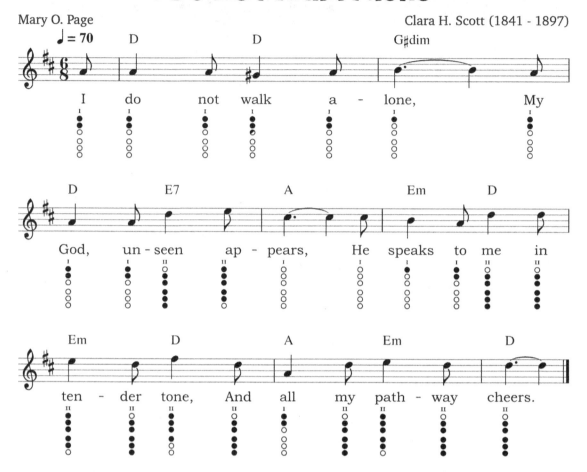

I do not walk alone, My God, unseen appears,
He speaks to me in tender tone, And all my pathway cheers.

I do not walk alone, His strength my strength shall be,
For I have claimed Him as my own, And found sweet liberty.

I do not walk alone, No more earth-bound I tread,
But swift on wings my life has flown; My soul, how comforted!

I do not walk alone, My joy I'd give to thee;
My brother, sister, claim thine own, And find sweet liberty.

Jesus Christ Is Passing By

J. Denham Smith (1817 - 1889)   Phoebe Knapp (1839 – 1908)

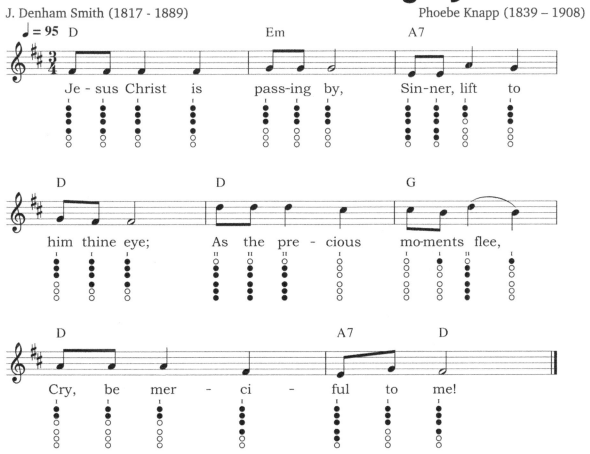

Jesus Christ is passing by,
Sinner, lift to him thine eye;
As the precious moments flee,
Cry, be merciful to me!

Lo! he stands and calls to thee,
"What wilt thou then have of me?"
Rise, and tell him all thy need;
Rise, he calleth thee indeed.

"Lord, I would thy mercy see;
Lord, reveal thy love to me;
Let it penetrate my soul,
All my heart and life control."

Oh, how sweet the touch of power
Comes, and is salvation's hour:
Jesus gives from guilt release,
"Faith hath saved thee, go in peace!"

Jesus, Dear, I Come to Thee

Fanny Crosby (1820 – 1915)

♪ = 110

Je - sus, dear, I come to thee, Thou hast said I
Je - sus, dear, I learn of thee, In thy word di -

may; Tell me what my life should be,
vine, Ev - 'ry prom - ise there I see,

Take my sins a - way. Je - sus, hear my hum - ble song,
May I call it mine.

I am weak, but thou art strong, Gen - tly lead my

soul a - long, Help me come to thee.

Jesus, dear, I come to thee,
Thou hast said I may;
Tell me what my life should be,
Take my sins away.
Jesus, dear, I learn of thee,
In thy word divine,
Ev'ry promise there I see,
May I call it mine.

Chorus:
Jesus, hear my humble song,
I am weak, but thou art strong,
Gently lead my soul along,
Help me come to thee.

Jesus, dear, I long for thee,
Long thy peace to know,
Grant those purer joys to me,
Earth can ne'er bestow;
Jesus, dear, I cling to thee;
When my heart is sad,
Thou wilt kindly speak to me,
Thou wilt make me glad.

Jesus, dear, I trust in thee,
Trust thy tender love,
There's a happy home for me,
With thy saints above;
Jesus, I would come to thee,
Thou hast said I may,
Tell me what my life should be,
Take my sins away.

Lift Up, O Little Children

Mary A. Lathbury (1841 - 1913)

Mary C. Seward (1839 – 1919)

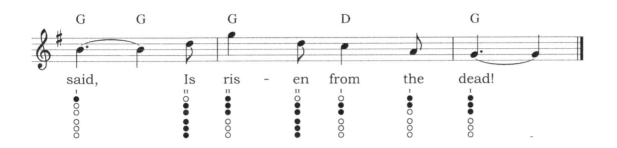

Lift up, O little children,
Your voices clear and sweet,
And sing the blessed story
Of Christ, the Lord of glory,
And worship at His feet,
And worship at His feet.

Refrain:
Oh, sing the blessed story!
The Lord of life and glory
Is risen, as He said,
Is risen from the dead!

Lift up, O tender lilies,
Your whiteness to the sun;
The earth is not our prison,
Since Christ Himself hath risen,
The life of ev'ry one,
The life of ev'ry one.

Ring, all ye bells of Easter,
Your chimes of joy again,
Ring out the night of sadness
Ring in the morn of gladness,
For death no more shall reign,
For death no more shall reign.

Multitudes, Multitudes

Eliza Edmunds Hewitt (1851 – 1920)

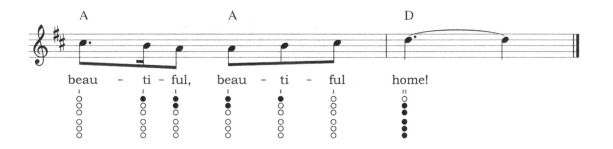

beau - ti - ful, beau - ti - ful home!

Beyond, just beyond the dark shadows of time,
A beautiful home, bright, beautiful home,
Stands blissful and radiant, in fair Summer-clime,
Our beautiful, beautiful home.

Refrain:
Multitudes, multitudes gathering there,
Numberless, numberless, spotless and fair,
Many the mansions our Lord will prepare,
O beautiful, beautiful home!

These earthly reunions are fleeting at best,
That beautiful home, bright, beautiful home,
Invites us to seek an eternity blest,
Our beautiful, beautiful home.

Its flowers, pure and fadeless, no winter will blight,
That beautiful home, bright, beautiful home,
No sin there, nor sorrow, no parting, no night,
Our beautiful, beautiful home.

Then onward, press on in the blood-sprinkled way;
That beautiful home, bright, beautiful home
Will open its bright, pearly portals some day,
O beautiful, beautiful home.

My Life is in Thee

Clara H. Scott (1841 - 1897)

My life is in Thee, Thou omnipresent One,
My life is in Thee, Thou omnipresent One.
Fountain of life Thou art, Springing within each heart,
No life from Thee apart, Thou Goodness divine!

My health is in Thee, Thou omnipresent One,
My health is in Thee, Thou omnipresent One.
All good I draw from Thee, Thy law preserveth me;
Help me this truth to see, And prove it divine.

All power is in Thee, Thou omnipresent One,
All power is in Thee, Thou omnipresent One.
Thus Error's chains are riven; Heir of the wealth of heav'n,
To me, His child, is given A freedom divine.

Now I Lay Me Down to Sleep

Mary Artemisia Lathbury (1841 - 1913)

46

Now I lay me down to sleep,
In Thy shadows soft and deep,
I pray Thee, Lord, my soul to keep,
I lay me, Lord,
Among Thy shadows
soft and dark and deep,
I pray Thee, Lord, A helpless soul
that leans on Thee, to keep.

If I should die before I wake,
For Thy unfailing mercy's sake,
I pray Thee, Lord, my soul to take.
If I should die
in some deep dream
and never here awake,
If I should die, I trust Thee, Lord,
my sleeping soul to take.

Omnipresence

Clara H. Scott (1841 - 1897)

Always with me! I can never
Stray beyond His tender care,
For our God is omnipresent,
Here and there and ev'rywhere,
Yes, ev'rywhere, and ev'rywhere,
Here and there and ev'rywhere.

Al-ways with me! Love so tender
Feels each trembling breath of pray'r,
For our God is ever list'ning,
And His love is ev'rywhere,
Yes, ev'rywhere,and ev'rywhere,
And His love is ev'rywhere.

Always with me! In His treasures,
Free, abundant, I may share,
For He holds them ever ready
For His children ev'rywhere,
Yes, ev'rywhere, and ev'rywhere,
For His children ev'rywhere.

Al-ways with me ! Ev'ry burden
His strong arm will help me bear,
For our God is omnipresent,
With His children ev'rywhere,
Yes, ev'rywhere, and ev'rywhere,
With His children ev'rywhere.

Open My Eyes, That I May See

Clara H. Scott (1841 – 1897)

Open my eyes that I may see
glimpses of truth thou hast for me.
Place in my hands the wonderful key
that shall unclasp and set me free.
Silently now I wait for thee,
ready, my God, thy will to see.
Open my eyes, illumine me,
Spirit divine!

Open my ears that I may hear
voices of truth thou sendest clear,
and while the wave notes fall on my ear,
ev'rything false will disappear.
Silently now I wait for thee,
ready, my God, thy will to see.
Open my ears, illumine me,
Spirit divine!

Open my mouth and let me bear
gladly the warm truth ev'rywhere.
Open my heart and let me prepare
love with thy children thus to share.
Silently now I wait for thee,
ready, my God, thy will to see.
Open my mouth, illumine me,
Spirit divine!

Promised Land

Samuel Stennett (1727 - 1795)

Matilda T. Durham (1815 – 1901)

On Jordan's storm-y banks I stand, and cast a wish-ful eye. to Cana-an's fair and hap - py land, where my pos - ses-sions lie. I am bound for the prom-ised land, I'm bound for the prom - ised land; oh, who will come and go with me? I am bound for the prom - ised land.

On Jordan's stormy banks I stand,
and cast a wishful eye
to Canaan's fair and happy land,
where my possessions lie.

Refrain:
I am bound for the promised land,
I am bound for the promised land;
oh, who will come and go with me?
I am bound for the promised land.

O'er all those wide extended plains
shines one eternal day;
there God the Son forever reigns,
and scatters night away.

No chilling winds or poisonous breath
can reach that healthful shore;
sickness and sorrow, pain and death,
are felt and feared no more.

When I shall reach that happy place,
I'll be forever blest,
for I shall see my Father's face,
and in his bosom rest.

Rejoice With Me

Clara H. Scott (1841 - 1897)

Rejoice with me! I've found the Way Christ Jesus made so clear,
Gone are the thorns of pain and sin Dispersed each doubt and fear;
"I am the Way, the Truth, the Life," Cried that blest Son divine,
"Then follow me, and perfect life Shall be forever thine."

Rejoice with me! I've found the Truth, Glad truth that sets me free,
God is my all; in Him I've found Health, peace and harmony.
O Christ, Thou art the Way, the Truth, Thou art the Life divine!
I'll follow Thee, and perfect life Shall be forever mine.

Rejoice with me! I've found the Life The Master came to prove;
'Tis God in me and I in God, Just resting in His love.
Oh, blest the Way, the Truth, the Life! Blest immortality!
Sing now my soul! Time's but a breath; We're in eternity.

Room at the Fountain

Margaret J. Harris (1865 - 1919)

I heard my loving Saviour say,
There's room at the fountain for me,
Come wash the stains of sin away,
There's room at the fountain for thee.

Refrain:
Room, room, yes, there is room,
Room at the fountain for thee,
Room, room, yes, there is room,
There's room at the fountain for thee.

He cleansed my heart from inbred sin,
There's room at the fountain for me,
And now He keeps me pure within,
There's room at the fountain for thee.

I'll praise Him while He gives me breath,
There's room at the fountain for me;
He saved me from an awful death,
There's room at the fountain for thee.

His blood was shed but once for all,
There's room at the fountain for me;
don't reject sweet Mercy's call,
There's room at the fountain for thee.

We'll sing with all the saints above,
There's room at the fountain for me;
And praise Him for redeeming love,
There's room at the fountain for thee.

Star of Columbia

Timothy Dwight (1752 – 1817)

Clara H. Scott (1841 - 1897)

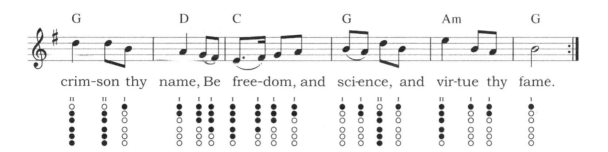

crim-son thy name, Be free-dom, and sci-ence, and vir-tue thy fame.

Columbia! Columbia! to glory arise,
The queen of the world, and the child of the skies,
Thy genius commands thee, with raptures behold,
While ages on ages thy splendors unfold:
Thy reign is the last and the noblest of time,
Most fruitful thy soil, most inviting thy clime;
Let crimes of the east ne'er encrimson thy name,
Be freedom, and science, and virtue thy fame.

To conquest and slaughter let Europe aspire,
Whelm nations in blood, or wrap cities in fire;
Thy heroes the rights of mankind shall defend,
And triumph pursue them and glory attend.
A world is thy realm, for a world be thy laws,
Enlarged as thy empire, and just as thy cause;
On freedom's broad basis that empire shall rise,
Extend with the main, and dissolve with the skies.

Fair science her gate to thy sons shall unbar,
And the east see thy morn hide the beams of her star;
New bards and new sages unrivalled shall soar
To fame unextinguished, when time is no more.
To the last refuge of virtue designed,
Shall fly from all nations, the best of mankind,
There, grateful to heaven, with transport shall bring
Their incense, more fragrant than odors of spring.

Nor less shall thy fair ones to glory ascend,
And genius and beauty in harmony blend;
Their graces of form shall awake pure desire,
And the charms of the soul still enliven the fire:
Their sweetness unmingled, their manners refined,
And virtue's bright image enstamped on the mind;
With peace and sweet rapture shall teach life to glow
And light up a smile in the aspect of woe.

Thy fleets to all regions thy power shall display
The nations admire, and the ocean obey;
Each shore to thy glory its tribute unfold,
And the east and the south yield their spices and gold,
As the day-spring unbounded thy splendors shall flow,
And earth's little kingdoms before thee shall bow,
While the ensigns of union in triumph unfurled,
Hush anarchy's sway, and give peace to the world.

Thus down a lone valley with cedars o'erspread,
From the noise of the town I pensively strayed,
The bloom from the face of fair heaven retired,
The wind ceased to murmur, the thunders expired
Perfumes, as of Eden, flowed sweetly along,
And a voice, as of angels, enchantingly sung,
Columbia! Columbia! to glory arise,
The queen of the world, and the child of the skies.

Sweet Rest in Jesus

Clara H. Scott (1841 - 1897)

There is sweet rest in Je - sus, For ev - 'ry trou - bled soul; There

is sweet rest in Je - sus, Whose word can make thee whole. Ye

need not groan 'neath bur - dens Up - on your soul hard

pressed, Lay down each un - solved ques - tion, And in Him be at

rest; Lay down each un - solved ques - tion, And in Him be at

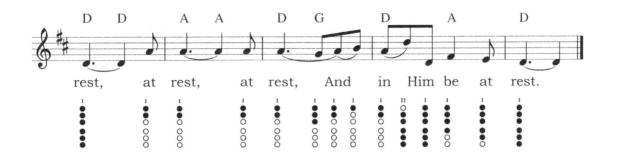

There is sweet rest in Jesus,
For ev'ry troubled soul;
There is sweet rest in Jesus,
Whose word can make thee whole.
Ye need not groan 'neath burdens
Upon your soul hard pressed,
Lay down each unsolved question,
And in Him be at rest;
Lay down each unsolved question,
And in Him be at rest,
At rest, at rest,
And in Him be at rest.

"Come unto me ye weary,"
Oh, hear the tender call!
"My peace I give unto thee,"
How sweet the accents fall.
No off'ring can y bring Him,
Save at His feet lay down
Your willing heart and giving,
Receive for naught, a crown;
Your willing heart and giving,
Receive for naught, a crown,
A crown, a crown,
Receive for naught a crown.

Why will ye not believe Him,
Ye sick and sore distressed?
Why will ye not receive Him
And be at peace and rest?
"Let not your heart be troubled,"
Amen, so let it be,
I lay my trembling hands in thine,
For all eternity;
I lay my trembling hands in thine,
For all eternity.
At rest, at rest,
For all eternity.

Tell It Out Among the Heathen

Frances R. Havergal (1836 - 1879)

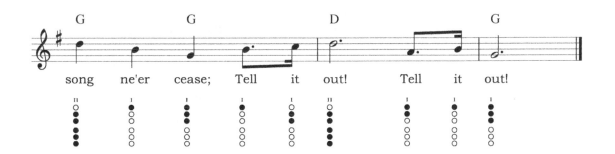

Tell it out among the heathen that the Lord is King;
Tell it out! Tell it out!
Tell it out among the nations, bid them shout and sing;
Tell it out! Tell it out!
Tell it out with adoration that He shall increase,
That the mighty King of Glory is the King of Peace;
Tell it out with jubilation, let the song ne'er cease;
Tell it out! Tell it out!

Tell it out among the heathen that the Savior reigns;
Tell it out! Tell it out!
Tell it out among the nations, bid them break their chains;
Tell it out! Tell it out!
Tell it out among the weeping ones that Jesus lives,
Tell it out among the weary ones what rest He gives,
Tell it out among the sinners that He still receives;
Tell it out! Tell it out!

Tell it out among the heathen, Jesus reigns above;
Tell it out! Tell it out!
Tell it out among the nations that His reign is love;
Tell it out! Tell it out!
Tell it out among the highways and the lanes at home,
Let it ring across the mountains and the ocean's foam,
Like the sound of many waters, let our glad shout come!
Tell it out! Tell it out!

That Grand Word, Whosoever

Eliza Edmunds Hewitt (1851 – 1920)

That grand word "who-so-ev – er" is ring-ing thro' my soul,

Who-so-ev – er will may come; In riv-ers of sal-va-tion the

liv-ing wa-ters roll, Who-so-ev – er will may come. O that

"who – so – ev – er"! Who-so-ev – er will may come; The

Sav-iour's in – vi-ta-tion is free – ly sound – ing still,

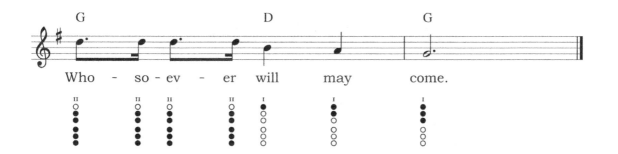

Who - so - ev - er will may come.

That grand word "whosoever" is ringing thro' my soul,
Whosoever will may come;
In rivers of salvation the living waters roll,
Whosoever will may come.

Refrain:
O that "whosoever"!
Whosoever will may come;
The Saviour's invitation is freely sounding still,
Whosoever will may come.

Whenever this sweet message in God's own word I see,
Whosoever will may come;
I know 'tis meant for sinners, I know 'tis meant for me,
Whosoever will may come.

I heard the loving message, and now to others say,
Whosoever will may come;
Seek now the precious Saviour, and he'll be yours today,
Whosoever will may come.

To God be all the glory! his only Son he gave,
Whosoever will may come;
And those who come believing, he'll to the utmost save,
Whosoever will may come.

Weary of Wandering

Mary C. Seward (1839 – 1919)

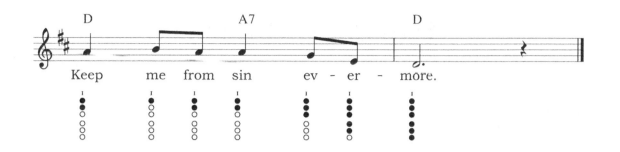

Weary of wandering from my Saviour,
Humbly again I'll seek his face,
Pleading his promises to save me,
Tasting again his pardoning grace.
Jesus, my Saviour, have mercy,
Freely forgive an restore;
Oh, for thy love have compassion,
Keep me from sin evermore.

Sinful, unworthy, but repenting,
Prostrate I bow before thy throne;
Seeking forgiveness and thy blessing,
Comfort and peace from thee alone.
Saviour, Redeemer, accept me,
Grant me thy presence and love;
Bear with my weakness and folly;
Send me thy strength from above.

Helpless I come, my sin confessing;
Trusting in thee, why need I fear,
Knowing that all so heavy-laden
Surely will find thee ever near?
Take, then, dear Saviour, my burden;
Teach me to walk in thy way;
Tenderly shelter and keep me;
Be thou my help and my stay.

Wonderful Peace

Eliza Edmunds Hewitt (1851 – 1920)

Jesus gives his peace to me,
Wonderful peace, wonderful peace;
Like his love, a boundless sea,
Wonderful, wonderful peace.

Refrain:
Peace, peace, wonderful peace,
Peace, peace, wonderful peace;
Jesus gives his peace to me,
Wonderful peace, wonderful peace.

Surface feelings ebb and flow,
Wonderful peace, wonderful peace;
Sweet, abiding calm below,
Wonderful peace, wonderful peace.

Not my charge his gift to hold,
Wonderful peace, wonderful peace;
Jesus keeps it–grace untold–
Wonderful peace, wonderful peace.

This my part–to trust in him,
Wonderful peace, wonderful peace;
Whether skies be bright or dim,
Wonderful peace, wonderful peace.

Praying, watching, serving still,
Wonderful peace, wonderful peace;
Let me learn, and do his will,
Wonderful peace, wonderful peace.

Appendix

Other Woman Composers of Old-Time Christian Music

I took some more time for this appendix. I presented some English hymn composers in the 19th century, known in England and the United States.

Charlotte Alington

Charlotte Alington (1830 - 1869), also known as Claribel, was a respected British composer and poet in the mid-19th century. Claribel's hymns are known for their melodic beauty and lyrical depth, often expressing her deep faith and devotion to God. Her compositions were renowned for their emotional sincerity and spiritual insight.

In addition to writing hymns, Claribel was a prolific composer of secular songs, ballads, and instrumental pieces. Her works were frequently performed in concerts and music halls, and her talent as a composer and poet earned her general recognition.

Despite personal challenges, including health and financial difficulties, Claribel continued composing and publishing music until her untimely death in 1869 at 39.

Frances Ridley Havergal

Frances Ridley Havergal (1836 - 1879) was an English hymn composer and writer. Despite fragile health, Havergal began writing poetry and hymns from a young age. Her first hymn was published when she was only 14 years old. In her relatively short life, she wrote hundreds of hymns, many still sung today.

Havergal's hymns were characterized by deep spiritual themes, personal devotion, and sincere expressions of faith. In addition to hymn writing, Havergal was a talented pianist, vocalist, and linguist. She traveled extensively, giving concerts, recitals, and lectures on various subjects, including music, literature, and theology.

Frances Ridley Havergal is remembered today as one of the most prolific and esteemed hymn writers of the 19th century. Her hymns are still sung in churches worldwide.

Sarah Geraldina Stock

Sarah Geraldina Stock (1839 - 1898) was an important composer of Christian songs in the 19th century. Her hymns are recognized for their lyrical beauty, profound messages, and rich theological content, reflecting her strong faith.

Sarah Geraldina Stock was also known for her deep compassion, and her hymns often reflected her heart for social justice and serving those in distress.

Sarah Geraldine Stock's hymns were published in various hymnals and songbooks during her lifetime, and her compositions are still cherished by Christians worldwide.

Children Prayer

Mary L. Duncan (1814 – 1840)

Charlotte Alington (1830 - 1869)

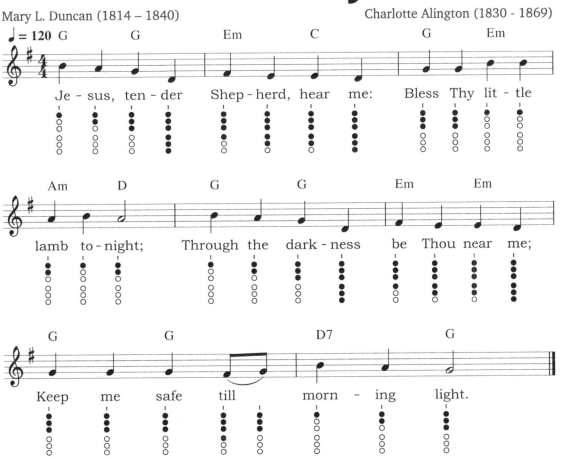

Jesus, tender Shepherd, hear me:
Bless Thy little lamb tonight;
Through the darkness be Thou near me;
Keep me safe till morning light.

All this day Thy hand has led me,
And I thank Thee for Thy care;
Thou hast warmed me, clothed and fed
Listen to my evening prayer!

Let my sins be all forgiven;
Bless the friends I love so well;
Take us all at last to heaven,
Happy there with Thee to dwell.

Golden Harps Are Sounding

Frances R. Havergal (1836 - 1879)

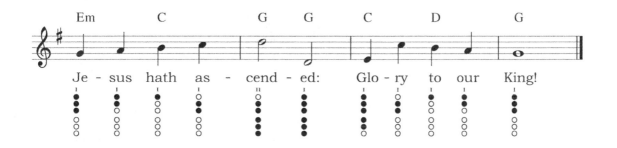

Golden harps are sounding,
Angel voices ring,
Pearly gates are opened,
Opened for the King:
Christ, the King of glory,
Jesus King of Love,
Is gone up in triumph
To His throne above.

Refrain:
All his work is ended,
Joyfully we sing:
Jesus hath ascended:
Glory to our King!

He who came to save us,
He who bled and died,
Now is crowned with glory
At His Father's side.
Nevermore to suffer,
Never more to die,
Jesus, King of Glory,
Is gone up on high.

Praying for his children
In that blessed place,
Calling them to glory,
Sending them His grace;
His bright home preparing,
Faithful ones, for you;
Jesus ever liveth,
Ever loveth too.

Jesus Calls

Sarah Geraldina Stock (1839 - 1898)

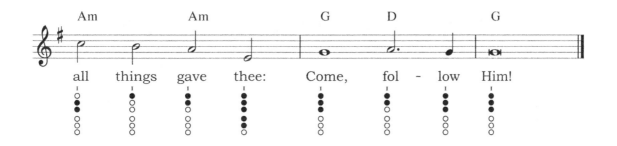

all things gave thee: Come, fol - low Him!

Jesus calls!
He it is who died to save thee;
He it is who all things gave thee;
Come, follow Him!
Come, thy ev'ry need confessing;
Come to Him for rest and blessing:
Trust, trust in Him!

Refrain:
Jesus calls!
He it is who died to save thee;
He it is who all things gave thee:
Come, follow Him!

Jesus calls!
Over highway, hill, and hollow—
Ev'rywhere He bids thee follow;
Yea, follow Him!
He will shield, uphold, and guide thee;
In His presence sweetly hide thee:
Trust, trust in Him!

Jesus calls!
There, where warfare He is waging,
And the angry foe is raging;
Come, follow Him!
With thy Captain onward leading,
Thou to victory art speeding:
Trust, trust in Him!

Let the Song Go Round the Earth

Sarah Geraldina Stock (1839 - 1898)

Let the song go round the earth,
Jesus Christ is Lord!
Sound His praises, tell His worth,
Be His Name adored;
Every clime and every tongue
Join the grand, the glorious song!

Let the song go round the earth!
From the eastern sea,
Where the daylight has its birth,
Glad, and bright, and free!
China's millions join the strains,
Waft them on to India's plains.

Let the song go round the earth!
Lands where Islam's sway
Darkly broods o'er home and hearth,
Cast their bonds away!
Let His praise from Afric's shore
Rise and swell her wide lands o'er!

Let the song go round the earth!
Where the summer smiles;
Let the notes of holy mirth
Break from distant isles!
Inland forests, dark and dim,
Icebound coasts give back the hymn.

Let the son go round the earth!
Jesus Christ is King!
With the story of His worth
Let the whole world ring!
Him creation all adore
Evermore and evermore!

O What Shall the Answer Be

Sarah Geraldina Stock (1839 - 1898)

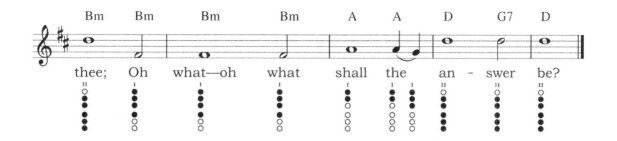

A cry, as of pain, again and again,
Is borne o'er the deserts and wide spreading main;
A cry from the lands that in darkness are lying,
A cry from the hearts that in sorrow are sighing;
It comes unto me; it comes unto thee;
Oh what—oh what shall the answer be?

Oh! hark to the call; it comes unto all
Whom Jesus hath rescued from sin's deadly thrall;
Come over and help us! in bondage we languish;
Come over and help us! we die in our anguish!;
It comes unto me; it comes unto thee;
Oh what—oh what shall the answer be?

It comes to the soul that Christ hath made whole,
The heart that is longing His name to extol;
It comes with a chorus of pitiful wailing;
It comes with a plea which is strong and prevailing;
For Christ's sake to me; For Christ's sake to thee;
Oh what—oh what shall the answer be?

We come, Lord, to Thee, Thy servants are we;
Inspire Thou the answer, and true it shall be!
If here we should work, or afar Thou should send us,
Oh grant that Thy mercy may ever attend us,
That each one may be a witness for Thee,
Till all the earth shall Thy glory see!

Someone Shall Go

Sarah Geraldina Stock (1839 - 1898)

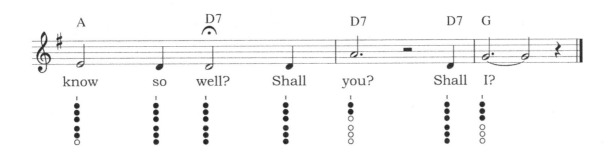

Someone shall go at the Master's word
Over the sea to the lands afar,
Telling to those who have never heard
What His wonderful mercies are.
Shall it be you—shall it be I?
Who shall haste to tell what we know so well?
Shall you? Shall I?

Someone shall gather the sheaves for Him,
Someone shall bind them with joyful hand,
Someone shall toil through the shadows dim,
For the morn in the heav'nly land.
Shall it be you—shall it be I?
Who shall bind the corn for the golden morn?
Shall you? Shall I?

Someone shall travel with eager feet
Over the mountain and through the wild,
Bringing the news of redemption sweet
To each wandering sinful child.
Shall it be you—shall it be I?
Who shall sound the tale over hill and dale?
Shall you? Shall I?

Someone shall carry His banner high,
Waving it out where the foe holds sway,
Some in His service shall live and die,
And with Jesus shall win the day!
Shall it be you— shall it be I?
Who His name shall bear, and His triumph share?
Shall you? Shall I?

The Tender Light of Home Behind

Sarah Geraldina Stock (1839 - 1898)

The ten - der light of home be - hind, Dark hea - then gloom be - fore, The ser - vants of the Lord go forth To many a for - eign shore: But the true light that can - not pale Streams on them from a - bove, A light di - vine, that

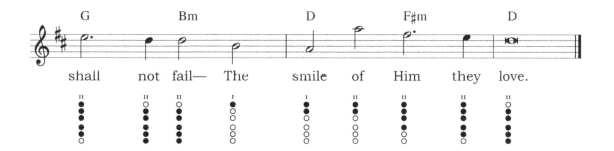

The tender light of home behind,
Dark heathen gloom before,
The servants of the Lord go forth
To many a foreign shore:
But the true light that cannot pale
Streams on them from above,
A light divine, that shall not fail—
The smile of Him they love.

The sheltering nest of home behind,
The battlefield before,
They gird their heav'nly armor on,
And seek the foreign shore:
But Christ their captain, with them goes,
He leads them in the way;
With Him they face the mightiest foes,
With Him they win the day.

The peaceful joys of home behind,
Danger and death before,
Right cheerfully they set their face
To seek the foreign shore:
For Christ has called, and His dear Word
Brings bliss, whate'er betide;
'Tis not alone—'tis with their Lord
They seek the other side.

A wealth of love and prayer behind,
Far-reaching hope before,
The servants of the Lord go forth
To seek a foreign shore:
And wheresoe'er their footsteps move
That hope makes sweet the air;
And all the path is paved with love,
And canopied with prayer.

Christ in the fondly-loved behind,
Christ in the bright before,
Oh! blest are they who start with Him
To seek the foreign shore!
Christ is their fair, unfading light,
Christ is their shield and sword,
Christ is their keeper, day and night,
And Christ their rich reward.

Used literature

Arthur, Alfred, Spirit of praise : a collection of music with hymns for use in Sabbath-school services and church meetings., Cleveland, Ohio : Ingham, Clarke & Co., 1882

B. Carradine, C. J. Fowler, W. J. Kirkpatrick, The Best of All: complete, Christian Witness Co., Chicago, Ill., 1910

Bell, Andrew, Songs of victory : a collection of hymns for evangelistic meetings, Christian worship, conferences, and the home circle, along with a selection of choruses, Glasgow : Scottish Bible and Book Society [etc.], 1890

D. B. Towner, J. Raymond Hemminger, Select Revival Hymns : a collection of new and old hymns suitable for every department of church work, Bible school, young people's societies, prayer meetings, evangelistic services, Y.M.C.A., Gospel Times Company, Carlisle, 1915

Dulles, John Welsh - Westminster Sabbath-School Hymnal: A Collection of Hymns and Tunes For Use in Sabbath-Schools and Social Meetings, Philadelphia : Presbyterian Board of Publication, 1883

Elderkin, George D, The Finest of the wheat : hymns new and old, for missionary and revival meetings, and Sabbath-schools, Chicago : R.R. McCabe & Co., 1890

Episcopal Church, The Church hymnal : revised and enlarged in accordance with the action of the General Convention of the Protestant Episcopal Church in the United States of America in the year of our Lord 1892 ; together with the morning and evening canticles (with the authorized pointing), Boston : The Parish Choir, 1894

Excell, E. O. (Edwin Othello), Triumphant songs no. 2, Chicago : E.O. Excell, 1889

Gold tried in the fire: suitable for church, Sunday school, revival meetings, missionary and rescue work, Indianapolis : Brown Brothers, 1904

Harris, George, Hymns of the faith with Psalms : for the use of congregations, Boston : Houghton, Mifflin, and Co., 1890

Ira D. Sankey, Winnowed Songs for Sunday Schools, Biglow & Main / The John Church Co., New York, 1890

Ira David, Sankey, Winnowed songs for Sunday schools, New York : Biglow & Main, 1890

James, J. S. (Joseph Summerlin), b. 1849, Union harp and history of songs : brief sketch of the authors of tunes and hymns ; newly arranged tune and song book consisting of sacred tunes, songs and anthems : prepared for churches, Sunday-schools, singing schools, conventions and all public gatherings as well as private classes and the home, Douglasville, Ga. : s.n.], 1909

Jenks, A. S., Devotional melodies, or a collection of original and selected tunes and hymns : designed for congregational and social worship /, Philadelphia : A. S. Jenks, 1859

Kirkpatrick, William J., Sunday-school praises : prepared especially for use in the Sunday-school, Cincinnati : Jennings & Pye ; New York : Eaton & Mains, 1900

Laymen's Missionary Movement of the United States and Canada, Laymen's Missionary Movement convention hymnal : with responsive readings, New York : Laymen's Missionary Movement, 1913

Life-Time Hymns: a collection of old and new hymns of the Christian Church (1896), p.57

Lowden, C. Harold, Miller, Rufus W. (Rufus Wilder), 1862-1925, Beginner and primary songs for use in Sunday school and the home, Philadelphia : Heidelberg Press, 1915

McDonald, W. (William), Beulah songs : a choice collection of popular hymns and music, new and old ; especially adapted to camp meetings, prayer and conference meetings, fami, Philadelphia : National Publishing Association for the Promotion of Holiness, 1879

Palmer, H. R., Life-time hymns;a collection of old and new hymns of the Christian church, for use in churches, Sunday-schools, prayer meetings and social gatherings, Chicago : R. R. McCabe & co., 1896.

Robinson, Charles S. (Charles Seymour), A Selection of spiritual songs with music : for the Sunday-School, New York : Century, 1881

Sayles, Harold F.; Hoffman, E. A. (Elisha Albright), Best hymns.for services of song in Christian work, Chicago : Evangelical Publishing Company, 1907

Scott, Clara H., Truth in song : for lovers of truth everywhere., Chicago : Mrs. Clara H. Scott, 1896

Seaborn McDaniel Denson, The Sacred Harp, James Edition Atlanta: n.p., 1911.

Seymour, Charles, A Selection of spiritual songs with music : for the Sunday-School, New York : Century, 1881

Snepp, Charles Busbridge, Songs of grace and glory, for private, family, and public worship. Ed. by C.B. Snepp., London: James Nisbet and Co., 1872

Sweney, John R. Et All, Songs of love and praise no. 4 : for use in meetings for Christian worship or work, Philadelphia : John J. Hood, 1897

Sweney, John R., 1837-1899; Kirkpatrick, William J., 1838-1921; Gilmour, H. L. (Henry Lake), 1836-1920, Praise in song : a collection of hymns and sacred melodies, adapted for use by Sunday schools, Endeavor societies, Epworth leagues, evangelists, pastors, choristers, etc., Philadelphia : John J. Hood, 1893

The Church Missionary Hymn Book, London : Church Missionary Society, 1899

Vail, S. J., Chapel melodies : a collection of choice hymns and tunes, both old and new, designed for the use of prayer and social meetings and family devotion ... New York : Biglow & Main, 1868

Walker, William, The Southern harmony, and musical companion : containing a choice collection of tunes, hymns, psalms, odes, and anthems ; selected from the most eminent authors in the United States ; together with nearly one hundred new tunes, which have never before been published ..., Philadelphia : E.W. Miller, 1847

William B. Bradbury, Sylvester Main, Cottage Melodies; a hymn and tune book, for prayer and social meetings and the home circle, Carlton & Porter, New York, 1859

Made in United States
Orlando, FL
06 September 2023